Christmas Carols

Christmas Carols

AVENEL BOOKS
New York

Copyright © 1990 by Outlet Book Company, Inc.

All rights reserved

First published in 1990 by Avenel Books,
distributed by Outlet Book Company, Inc.,
a Random House Company,
225 Park Avenue South,
New York, New York 10003

Manufactured in Italy

Edited by Glorya Hale
Designed by Melissa Ring

Library of Congress Cataloging-in-Publication Data

Christmas Carols.
1. Carols, English.   2. Christmas music.
M2110.C552   1990   90-751766
ISBN 0-517-02535-3

8   7   6   5   4   3   2   1

Contents

Introduction	7
All Through the Night	8
Angels, From the Realms of Glory	10
Away in a Manger	12
A Child This Day is Born	14
Coventry Carol	16
Deck the Hall	18
The First Noël	20
The Friendly Beasts	22
Go Tell it On the Mountain	24
God Rest You Merry, Gentlemen	26
Good King Wenceslas	28
Hark! The Herald Angels Sing	30
The Holly and the Ivy	32
I Heard the Bells on Christmas Day	34
It Came Upon the Midnight Clear	36
Jolly Old Saint Nicholas	38
Joy to the World	40
O Christmas Tree	42
O Come, All Ye Faithful	44
O Little Town of Bethlehem	46
The Old Year Now Away is Fled	48
Pat-a-Pan	50
Silent Night	52
Three Kings of Orient	54
The Wassail Song	56
We Wish You a Merry Christmas	58
What Child is This?	60
While Shepherds Watched Their Flocks	62

Introduction

Christmas is a special time, a time of gift-giving and merriment, of reflection and renewal. It is a time when children and grown-ups go out caroling and friends and families gather around the piano to sing of the season's wonders and joys.

Many of the Christmas carols in this new collection are traditional favorites. Some may be less familiar. Included are songs from many countries, from Germany, Wales, France, England, and Italy, as well as from the United States. One carol, "I Heard the Bells on Christmas Day," is a poem by Henry Wadsworth Longfellow which has been set to music. The words to another carol, "Joy to the World," were written by the British poet Isaac Watts; the music was written by the famous composer George Frederick Handel. "O Come All Ye Faithful" is a translation of an old Latin hymn and "Go Tell it On the Mountain" is an African-American spiritual. Two of the carols in this collection, "The Old Year Now Away is Fled" and "What Child Is This?" are set to the music of the lovely "Greensleeves."

Most of these carols celebrate the Christmas holiday. A few of them welcome the new year. All of them have been chosen to reflect the spirit and meaning of the season and to delight everyone who sings them.

7

All Through the Night

Sleep, my love, and peace attend thee
    all through the night,
Guardian angels God will lend thee
    all through the night.
Soft the drowsy hours are creeping
Hill and vale in slumber sleeping,
Love alone His watch is keeping
    all through the night.

All Through the Night

Welsh

Sleep, my love, and peace at-tend thee all through the night.

Guard - ian an-gels God will lend thee all through the night.

Soft the drow-sy hours are creep-ing, Hill and vale in slum-ber sleep-ing,

Love a-lone His watch is keep-ing all through the night.

Angels, From the Realms of Glory

Angels, from the realms of glory,
   Wing your flight o'er all the earth;
Ye, who sang creation's story,
   Now proclaim Messiah's birth.
      Come and worship! Come and worship!
      Worship Christ the newborn King!

Shepherds, in the fields abiding,
   Watching o'er your flocks by night,
God with man is now residing,
   Yonder shines the infant light.
      Come and worship! Come and worship!
      Worship Christ the newborn King!

Sages, leave your contemplations,
   Brighter visions beam afar;
Seek the great Desire of nations,
   Ye have seen his natal star.
      Come and worship! Come and worship!
      Worship Christ the newborn King!

All creation, join in praising
   God, the Father, Spirit, Son,
Evermore your voices raising
   To the eternal Three in One.
      Come and worship! Come and worship!
      Worship Christ the newborn King!

Angels, From the Realms of Glory

An-gels from the realms of glo-ry, Wing your flight o'er all the earth;

Ye who sang cre - a - tion's sto-ry, Now pro claim Mes - si - ah's birth.

Come and wor-ship! Come and wor ship! Wor-ship Christ the new-born King!

Away in a Manger

Away in a manger, no crib for a bed,
  The little Lord Jesus laid down his sweet head.
The stars in the sky looked down where he lay,
  The little Lord Jesus asleep in the hay.

The cattle are lowing, the baby awakes,
  But little Lord Jesus no crying he makes.
I love Thee, Lord Jesus, look down from the sky
  And stay by my side 'til morning is nigh.

Be near me, Lord Jesus, I ask Thee to stay
  Close by me forever, and love me, I pray.
Bless all the dear children in thy tender care,
  And fit us for heaven, to live with Thee there.

Away in a Manger

German

A - way in a man - ger, no crib for a
bed, The lit - tle Lord Je - sus laid down his sweet
head; The stars in the sky looked down where he
lay, The lit - tle Lord Je - sus a - sleep in the hay.

A Child This Day is Born

A child this day is born,
   A child of high renown,
Most worthy of a scepter,
   A scepter and a crown:

Noël, Noël, Noël,
   Noël, sing all we may,
Because the King of all kings
   Was born this blessed day.

These tidings shepherds heard,
   In field watching their fold,
Were by an angel unto them
   That night revealed and told:

To whom the angel spoke,
   Saying, "Be not afraid;
Be glad, poor silly shepherds—
   Why are you so dismayed?"

"For lo! I bring you tidings
   Of gladness and of mirth,
Which cometh to all people by
   This holy infant's birth."

Then was there with the angel
   An host incontinent
Of heavenly bright soldiers,
   Which from the Highest was sent:

Lauding the Lord our God,
   And His celestial King;
All glory be in Paradise,
   This heavenly host did sing:

And as the angel told them,
   So to them did appear;
They found the young Child,
     Jesus Christ,
   With Mary, His Mother dear:

A Child This Day is Born

Traditional

A child this day is— born,— A child of high— re -
nown, Most wor-thy of a scep-ter, A scep-ter and a

Chorus

crown: No -el, No-el, No -el, No -el, sing all— we—
may, Be -cause the King of all— kings Was born this bless-ed day.

Coventry Carol

Lullay, Thou little tiny Child
  By by, lully, lullay.
Lullay, Thou little tiny Child,
  By by, lully, lullay.

O sisters too, how may we do,
  For to preserve this day.
This poor youngling for whom we sing
  By by, lully, lullay.

Herod the king, in his raging,
  Charged he hath this day.
His men of might, in his own sight,
  All young children to slay.

That woe is me, poor Child for Thee!
  And ever morn and day,
For Thy parting neither say nor sing
  By by, lully, lullay!

 16

Coventry Carol

Traditional

p Lul - lay, Thou lit - tle ti - ny Child,

cresc. By by, lul - lay, lul - lay,_____ *mf* Lul -

lay, Thou lit - tle ti - ny Child, *dim.*

pp By by, lul - lay, lul - lay._____ *rall.*

Deck the Hall

Deck the hall with boughs of holly,
Fa la la la la, la la la la.
'Tis the season to be jolly,
Fa la la la la, la la la la.
Don we now our gay apparel,
Fa la la, la la la, la la la.
Troll the ancient Yuletide carol,
Fa la la la la, la la la la.

See the blazing yule before us,
Fa la la la la, la la la la.
Strike the harp and join the chorus.
Fa la la la la, la la la la.
Follow me in merry measure,
Fa la la, la la la, la la la.
While I tell of Yuletide treasure,
Fa la la la la, la la la la.

Fast away the old year passes,
Fa la la la la, la la la la.
Hail the new, ye lads and lasses,
Fa la la la la, la la la la.
Sing we joyous, all together,
Fa la la, la la la, la la la.
Heedless of the wind and weather,
Fa la la la la, la la la la.

Deck the Hall

Welsh

Deck the hall with boughs of hol-ly, Fa la la la la, la la la la.

'Tis the sea-son to be jol-ly, Fa la la la la, la la la la.

Don we now our gay ap-par-el, Fa la la la la la la la la.

Troll the an-cient Yule-tide car-ol, Fa la la la la, la la la la.

The First Noël

The first Noël, the angel did say,
Was to certain poor shepherds in fields as they lay;
In fields where they lay keeping their sheep,
On a cold winter's night that was so deep.
   Noël, Noël, Noël, Noël,
   Born is the King of Israel.

They looked up and saw a star
Shining in the East, beyond them far;
And to the earth it gave great light,
And so it continued both day and night.
   Noël, Noël, Noël, Noël,
   Born is the King of Israel.

And by the light of that same star,
Three wise men came from country far;
To seek for a King was their intent,
And to follow the star wherever it went.
   Noël, Noël, Noël, Noël,
   Born is the King of Israel.

This star drew night to the northwest,
O'er Bethlehem it took its rest;
And there it did both stop and stay,
Right over the place where Jesus lay.
   Noël, Noël, Noël, Noël,
   Born is the King of Israel.

Then entered in those wise men three,
Full reverently upon their knee;
And offered there in His presence,
Their gold, and myrrh, and frankincense.
   Noël, Noël, Noël, Noël,
   Born is the King of Israel.

The First Noël

The Friendly Beasts

Jesus our brother, kind and good
   Was humbly born in a stable rude,
And the friendly beasts around Him stood,
   Jesus our brother, kind and good.

"I," said the donkey, shaggy and brown,
   "I carried His mother up hill and down;
I carried her safely to Bethlehem town."
   "I," said the donkey, shaggy and brown.

"I," said the cow all white and red
   "I gave Him my manger for His bed;
I gave Him my hay to pillow his head."
   "I," said the cow all white and red.

"I," said the sheep with curly horn,
   "I gave Him my wool for His blanket warm;
He wore my coat on Christmas morn."
   "I," said the sheep with curly horn.

"I," said the dove from the rafters high,
   "I cooed Him to sleep so He would not cry;
We cooed him to sleep, my mate and I."
   "I," said the dove from the rafters high.

Thus every beast by some good spell,
   In the stable dark was glad to tell
Of the gift he gave Immanuel,
   The gift he gave Immanuel.

The Friendly Beasts

English

Je - sus our broth - er, kind and good Was hum - bly born in a sta - ble rude, And the friend - ly beasts a - round Him stood, Je - sus our broth - er, kind and good.

Go Tell it On the Mountain

When I was a seeker
  I sought both night and day,
I asked the Lord to help me,
  And He showed me the way.

Go tell it on the mountain,
  Over the hills and everywhere,
Go tell it on the mountain
  Our Jesus Christ is born.

He made me a watchman
  Upon a city wall,
And if I am a Christian,
  I am the least of all.

Go tell it on the mountain,
  Over the hills and everywhere,
Go tell it on the mountain
  Our Jesus Christ is born.

Go Tell it On the Mountain

Spiritual

When I was a seek-er I sought both night and day, I asked the Lord to help me, And He showed me the way.

Chorus

Go tell it on the moun-tain, O-ver the hills and ev-'ry where;

Go tell it on the moun-tain, Our Je-sus Christ— is born.

God Rest You Merry, Gentlemen

God rest you merry, gentlemen,
　Let nothing you dismay,
Remember Christ our Savior
　Was born on Christmas day,
To save us all from Satan's pow'r
　When we were gone astray;
　　O *tidings of comfort and joy,*
　　　Comfort and joy,
　　O *tidings of comfort and joy.*

From God our heavenly Father
　A blessed angel came.
And unto certain shepherds
　Brought tidings of the same,
How that in Bethlehem was born
　The Son of God by name:
　　O *tidings of comfort and joy,*
　　　Comfort and joy,
　　O *tidings of comfort and joy.*

"Fear not," then said the angel,
　"Let nothing you affright,
This day is born a Savior,
　Of virtue, power, and might;
So frequently to vanquish all
　The friends of Satan quite";
　　O *tidings of comfort and joy,*
　　　Comfort and joy,
　　O *tidings of comfort and joy.*

The shepherds at those tidings
　Rejoiced much in mind,
And left their flocks a-feeding,
　In tempest, storm, and wind,
And went to Bethlehem straightway
　This blessed babe to find:
　　O *tidings of comfort and joy,*
　　　Comfort and joy,
　　O *tidings of comfort and joy.*

But when to Bethlehem they came,
　Whereat this infant lay
They found him in a manger,
　Where oxen feed on hay;
His mother Mary kneeling,
　Unto the Lord did pray:
　　O *tidings of comfort and joy,*
　　　Comfort and joy,
　　O *tidings of comfort and joy.*

Now to the Lord sing praises,
　All you within this place,
And with true love and brotherhood
　Each other now embrace;
This holy tide of Christmas
　All others doth deface:
　　O *tidings of comfort and joy,*
　　　Comfort and joy,
　　O *tidings of comfort and joy.*

26

God Rest You Merry, Gentlemen

Traditional

Good King Wenceslas

Good King Wenceslas looked out,
  On the Feast of Stephen,
When the snow lay round about,
  Deep and crisp and even;
Brightly shone the moon that night,
  Tho' the frost was cruel,
When a poor man came in sight,
  Gath'ring winter fuel.

"Hither, page, and stand by me,
  If thou know'st it, telling,
Yonder peasant, who is he?
  Where and what his dwelling?"
"Sire, he lives a good league hence,
  Underneath the mountain;
Right against the forest fence,
  By Saint Agnes' fountain."

"Bring me flesh, and bring me wine,
  Bring me pine logs hither:
Thou and I will see him dine,
  When we bear them thither."
Page and monarch, forth they went,
  Forth they went together;
Thro' the rude wind's wild lament
  And the bitter weather.

"Sire, the night is darker now,
  And the wind blows stronger;
Fails my heart, I know not how,
  I can go no longer."
Mark my footsteps, good my page;
  Tread thou in them boldly:
Thou shalt find the winter's rage
  Freeze thy blood less coldly."

In his master's steps he trod,
  Where the snow lay dinted;
Heat was in the very sod
  Which the saint had printed.
Therefore, Christian men, be sure,
  Wealth or rank possessing,
Ye who now will bless the poor,
  Shall yourselves find blessing.

Good King Wenceslas

John Mason Neale

Latin

Good King Wen-ces - las looked out, On the feast of Ste - phen,

When the snow lay round a - bout, Deep, and crisp and ev - en:

Bright-ly shone the moon that night, Tho' the frost was cru - el,

When a poor man came in sight, Gath-'ring win-ter fu - el.

Hark! The Herald Angels Sing

Hark! the herald angels sing,—
"Glory to the newborn King!
Peace on earth, and mercy mild,
God and sinners reconciled."
Joyful, all ye nations, rise,
Join the triumph of the skies;
With th' angelic host proclaim,
"Christ is born in Bethlehem."
Hark! the herald angels sing,
"Glory to the newborn King!"

Christ, by highest heav'n adored:
Christ the everlasting Lord;
Late in time behold him come,
Offspring of the favored one.
Veil'd in flesh, the Godhead see;
Hail, th'incarnate Deity:
Pleased, as man, with men to dwell,
Jesus, our Immanuel!
Hark! the herald angels sing,
"Glory to the newborn King!"

Hail! the heav'n-born Prince of peace!
Hail! the Son of Righteousness!
Light and life to all he brings,
Risen with healing in his wings
Mild he lays his glory by,
Born that man no more may die:
Born to raise the sons of earth,
Born to give them second birth.
Hark! the herald angels sing,
"Glory to the newborn King!"

Hark! The Herald Angels Sing

Charles Wesley   **Felix Mendelssohn**

Hark! the her-ald an-gels sing,— "Glo-ry to the new-born King!

Peace on earth, and mer-cy mild,— God and sin-ners re-con-ciled."

Joy-ful, all ye na-tions, rise,— Join the tri-umph of the skies;—

With th' an-gel-ic host pro-claim, "Christ is— born in Beth-le-hem."

Hark! the her-ald an-gels sing, "Glo-ry— to the new-born King!"

The Holly and the Ivy

The holly and the ivy,
    When they are both full grown,
Of all the trees that are in the wood,
    The holly bears the crown.

O the rising of the sun,
    And the running of the deer,
The playing of the merry organ,
    Sweet singing in the choir.

The holly bears a blossom
    As white as lily flower;
And Mary bore sweet Jesus Christ
    To be our sweet Savior.

The holly bears a berry
    As red as any blood;
And Mary bore sweet Jesus Christ
    To do poor sinners good.

The holly bears a prickle
    As sharp as any thorn;
And Mary bore sweet Jesus Christ
    On Christmas day in the morn.

The holly bears a bark
    As bitter as any gall;
And Mary bore sweet Jesus Christ
    For to redeem us all.

The holly and the ivy
    When they are both full grown,
Of all the trees that are in the wood,
    The holly bears the crown.

The Holly and the Ivy

Traditional

The hol-ly and the i-vy, When they are both full-grown, Of all the trees that are in the wood, The hol-ly bears the crown.

Chorus

O the ris-ing of the sun, And the run-ning of the deer, The play-ing of the mer-ry or-gan, Sweet sing-ing in the choir.

I Heard the Bells on Christmas Day

I heard the bells on Christmas day
Their old familiar carols play
And mild and sweet the words repeat,
Of peace on earth, good will to men.

I thought how as the day had come,
The belfries of all Christendom
Had roll'd along th' unbroken song
Of peace on earth, good will to men.

And in despair I bow'd my head:
"There is no peace on earth," I said,
"For hate is strong, and mocks the song
Of peace on earth, good will to men."

Then pealed the bells more loud and deep:
"God is not dead, nor doth He sleep;
The wrong shall fail, the right prevail,
With peace on earth, good will to men."

'Til, ringing, singing on its way,
The world revolved from night to day,
A voice, a chime, a chant sublime,
Of peace on earth, good will to men!

I Heard the Bells on Christmas Day

Henry Wadsworth Longfellow

John Baptiste Calkin

I heard the bells on Christ - mas day Their old fa-mil-iar car - ols play And

mild and sweet the words re-peat, Of peace on earth, good will to men.

It Came Upon the Midnight Clear

It came upon the midnight clear,
   That glorious song of old,
From angels bending near the earth
   To touch their harps of gold!
"Peace on the earth, good will to men,
   From heaven's all gracious King!"
The world in solemn stillness lay
   To hear the angels sing.

Still through the cloven skies they come
   With peaceful wings unfurled
And still their heavenly music floats
   O'er all the weary world;
Above its sad and lowly plains
   They bend on hovering wing.
And ever o'er its Babel sounds
   The blessed angels sing.

Yet with the woes of sin and strife
   The world hath suffered long;
Beneath the angel-strain have rolled
   Two thousand years of wrong;
And man, at war with man, hears not
   The love song which they bring:
O hush the noise, ye men of strife,
   And hear the angels sing.

For lo! the days are hastening on,
   By prophet bards foretold,
When, with the ever-circling years,
   Shall come the Age of Gold;
When peace shall over all the earth
   Its ancient splendors fling,
And all the world give back the song
   Which now the angels sing.

It Came Upon the Midnight Clear

Edmund H. Sears

Richard S. Willis

It came up-on a mid-night clear, That glo-rious song of old, From an-gels bend-ing near the earth To touch their harps of gold! "Peace on the earth good will to men, From heav-en's all gra-cious King! The world in sol-emn still-ness lay To hear the an-gels sing.

Jolly Old Saint Nicholas

Jolly old Saint Nicholas,
    Lean your ear this way!
Don't you tell a single soul
    What I'm going to say;
Christmas Eve is coming soon;
    Now, you dear old man,
Whisper what you'll bring to me;
    Tell me if you can.

When the clock is striking twelve,
    When I'm fast asleep,
Down the chimney broad and black,
    With your pack you'll creep;
All the stockings you will find
    Hanging in a row;
Mine will be the shortest one,
    You'll be sure to know.

Johnny wants a pair of skates;
    Susy wants a dolly;
Nellie wants a story book;
    She think dolls are folly;
As for me, my little brain
    Isn't very bright;
Choose for me, old Santa Claus,
    What you think is right.

Jolly Old Saint Nicholas

Traditional

Jol - ly old Saint Nich - o - las, Lean your ear this way!

Don't you tell a sin-gle soul What I'm going to say;

Christ - mas Eve is com-ing soon; Now, you dear old man,

Whis - per what you'll bring to me; Tell me if you can.

Joy to the World

Joy to the world! The Lord is come:
   Let earth receive her King.
Let ev'ry heart prepare Him room,
   And heaven and nature sing,
   And heaven and nature sing,
   And heaven and heaven and nature sing.

He rules the world with truth and grace,
   And makes the nations prove
The glories of His righteousness
   And wonders of His love,
   And wonders of His love,
   And wonders, wonders of His love.

Joy to the World

Isaac Watts

George F. Handel

O Christmas Tree

O Christmas tree, O Christmas tree!
  How are thy leaves so verdant!
O Christmas tree, O Christmas tree
  How are thy leaves so verdant!

Not only in the summertime,
  But e'en in winter is thy prime.
O Christmas tree, O Christmas tree!
  How are thy leaves so verdant!

O Christmas tree, O Christmas tree,
  Much pleasure doth thou bring me!
O Christmas tree, O Christmas tree,
  Much pleasure doth thou bring me!

For every year the Christmas tree,
  Brings to us all both joy and glee.
O Christmas tree, O Christmas tree,
  Much pleasure doth thou bring me!

O Christmas tree, O Christmas tree,
  Thy candles shine out brightly!
O Christmas tree, O Christmas tree,
  Thy candles shine out brightly!

Each bough doth hold its tiny light,
  That makes each toy to sparkle bright.
O Christmas tree, O Christmas tree
  Thy candles shine out brightly!

O Christmas Tree

Traditional

O Christ-mas tree, O Christ-mas tree! How are thy leaves so

ver - dant! O Christ-mas tree, O Christ-mas tree! How are thy leaves so

ver - dant! *f* Not on - ly in the sum - mer - time, But

e'en in win - ter is thy prime. *mf* O Christ - mas tree, O

Christ - mas tree! *dim.* How are thy leaves so ver - dant!

O Come, All Ye Faithful

O come, all ye faithful,
    Joyful and triumphant,
O come ye, O come ye to Bethlehem.
    Come and behold Him,
Monarch of Angels!
    O come, let us adore Him,
    O come, let us adore Him,
    O come, let us adore Him,
        Christ the Lord.

Sing, alleluia,
    All ye choirs of angels;
O sing, all ye blissful ones of Heav'n above.
    Glory to God—
In the highest glory!
    O come, let us adore Him,
    O come, let us adore Him,
    O come, let us adore Him,
        Christ the Lord.

Yea, Lord, we greet Thee,
    Born this happy morning;
Jesus, to Thee be the glory giv'n;
    Word of the Father,
Now in the flesh appearing,
    O come, let us adore Him,
    O come, let us adore Him,
    O come, let us adore Him,
        Christ the Lord.

O Come, All Ye Faithful

J. Reading

O Little Town of Bethlehem

O little town of Bethlehem,
   How still we see thee lie;
Above thy deep and dreamless sleep
   The silent stars go by;
Yet in thy dark streets shineth
   The everlasting light.
The hopes and fears of all the years
   Are met in thee tonight.

For Christ is born of Mary,
   And gathered all above,
While mortals sleep the angels keep
   Their watch of wond'ring love.
O morning stars, together
   Proclaim the holy birth!
And praises sing to God the King,
   And peace to men on earth!

O Little Town of Bethlehem

Phillips Brooks

Lewis H. Redner

O lit-tle town of Beth-le-hem! How still we — see thee lie; A-
bove thy deep and dream-less sleep The si-lent — stars go by; Yet
in thy dark streets shin — eth The ev-er last-ing light. The
hopes and fears of all the years Are met in thee to-night.

The Old Year Now Away is Fled

The old year now away is fled,
  The new year now is entered;
Then let us now our sins downtread,
  And joyfully all appear.
Merry be the holiday,
  And let us run with sport and play,
Hang sorrow, cast care away,
  God send you a Happy New Year!

And now with new year's gifts each friend
  Unto each other they do send;
God grant we may our lives amend,
  And that the truth may appear.
Like the snake cast off your skin
  Of evil thoughts and wicked sin,
To amend this new year begin,
  God send us a Merry New Year!

The Old Year Now Away is Fled

(Greensleeves)

Traditional

The old year now a-way is fled, The new year now is en-ter-ed; Then let us now our sins down-tread, And joy-ful-ly all ap-pear. Mer-ry be the hol-i-day, And let us run with sport and play, Hang sor-row, cast care a-way, God send you a hap-py new year!

Pat-a-Pan

Willie, bring your little drum;
Robin, bring your fife and come;
And be merry while you play,
   Tu - re - lu - re - lu,
   Pat - a - pat - a - pan,
Come be merry while you play,
Let us make our Christmas gay!

When the men of olden days
To the King of Kings gave praise,
On the fife and drum did play,
   Tu - re - lu - re - lu,
   Pat - a - pat - a - pan,
On the fife and drum did play,
So their hearts were glad and gay!

God and man today become
More in tune than fife and drum,
So be merry while you play,
   Tu - re - lu - re - lu,
   Pat - a - pat - a - pan,
So be merry while you play,
Sing and dance this Christmas gay!

Pat-a-Pan

French

Wil - lie, bring your lit - tle drum; Ro - bin, bring your

fife and come; And be mer - ry while you

play, Tu - re - lu - re - lu, Pat - a - pat - a - pan, Come be

mer - ry while you play, Let us make our Christ - mas gay!

Silent Night

Silent night, holy night!
  All is calm, all is bright.
Round yon Virgin, Mother and Child.
  Holy infant so tender and mild,
Sleep in heavenly peace,
  Sleep in heavenly peace.

Silent night, holy night!
  Shepherds quake at the sight.
Glories stream from heaven afar
  Heavenly hosts sing Alleluia,
Christ the Savior is born!
  Christ the Savior is born.

Silent night, holy night!
  Son of God love's pure light.
Radiant beams from Thy holy face
  With the dawn of redeeming grace,
Jesus Lord, at Thy birth.
  Jesus Lord at Thy birth.

 52

Silent Night

Joseph Mohr   Franz Gruber

Three Kings of Orient

We three kings of Orient are,
   Bearing gifts we traverse far
Field and fountain, moor and mountain,
   Following yonder Star.

O, star of wonder, star of might,
   Star with royal beauty bright,
Westward leading, still proceeding,
   Guide us to the perfect light.

Born a babe on Bethlehem's plain,
   Gold we bring to crown Him again;
King forever, ceasing never,
   Over us all to reign.

Frankincense to offer have I;
   Incense owns a Deity nigh;
Pray'r and praising, all men raising,
   Worship Him, God on High.

Myrrh is mine; its bitter perfume
   Breathes a life of gathering gloom;
Sorrowing, sighing, bleeding, dying,
   Seal'd in the stone-cold tomb.

Glorious now behold Him rise,
   King and God and sacrifice,
Heav'n sings, "Hallelujah!"
   "Hallelujah!" Earth replies.

Three Kings of Orient

Traditional

We three kings of Or - i - ent are, Bear-ing gifts we tra - verse—

far Field and foun-tain, moor and moun-tain, Fol - low - ing

Chorus

yon - der Star. Oh,— star of won - der, star of might,

Star with roy - al beau - ty bright, West - ward lead - ing,

still pro - ceed - ing, Guide us to the per - fect light.

The Wassail Song

Here we come a-wassailing
    Among the leaves so green,
Here we come a wand'ring,
    So fair to be seen.

Love and joy come to you,
    And to you your wassail too,
And God bless you and send you a happy new year,
    And God send you a happy new year.

We are not daily beggars
    Who beg from door to door,
But we are neighbor's children
    Whom you have seen before.

We have a little purse
    Made of ratching leather skin;
We want some of your small change
    To line it well within.

God bless the Master of this house,
    Likewise the Mistress too;
And all the little children
    That round the table go.

The Wassail Song

Traditional

Here we— come a was-sail-ing A-mong the leaves so green,— Here we come a wand-'ring, So fair— to be seen.

Chorus

f Love and joy come to you, And to you your was-sail too, And God bless you and send— you a hap-py new year,— And God send you a hap-py new— year.

We Wish You a Merry Christmas

We wish you a Merry Christmas,
We wish you a Merry Christmas,
We wish you a Merry Christmas,
  And a Happy New Year.

We all know that Santa's coming,
We all know that Santa's coming.
We all know that Santa's coming,
  And soon will be here.

Good tidings to you,
And all of your kin,
Good tidings for Christmas,
And a Happy New Year.

Good tidings to you,
And all of your kin,
Good tidings for Christmas,
And a Happy New Year.

We wish you a Merry Christmas,
We wish you a Merry Christmas,
We wish you a Merry Christmas
And a Happy New Year.

We Wish You a Merry Christmas

English

We wish you a Mer-ry Christ-mas, We wish you a Mer-ry
Christ-mas; We wish you a Mer-ry Christ-mas, And a Hap-py New

Chorus

Year! Good ti-dings to you, And all of your
kin, Good ti-dings for Christ-mas, And a Hap-py New Year.

What Child is This?

What child is this, who, laid to rest
    On Mary's lap, is sleeping?
Whom angels greet with anthems sweet,
    While shepherds watch are keeping?
This, this is Christ the King,
    Whom shepherds guard and angels sing:
Haste, haste to bring him laud,
    The Babe, the Son of Mary!

So bring Him incense, gold, and myrrh,
    Come peasant king to own Him,
The King of kings, salvation brings,
    Let loving hearts enthrone Him.
Raise, raise the song on high,
    The Virgin sings her lullaby:
Joy, joy, for Christ is born,
    The Babe, the Son of Mary!

What Child is This?

(Greensleeves)

Traditional

What child is this, who, laid to rest. On Ma-ry's lap is sleep- ing? Whom

an - gels greet with an - thems sweet While shep - herds watch are keep- ing?

This, this is Christ the King, Whom shep-herds guard and an - gels sing:

Haste, haste to bring him laud, The babe, the son of Ma - ry.

While Shepherds Watched Their Flocks

While shepherds watched their flocks by night,
   All seated on the ground,
The angel of the Lord came down,
   And glory shone around,
     And glory shone around.

"Fear not!" said He, for mighty dread
   Had seized their troubled mind,
"Glad tidings of great joy I bring,
   To you and all mankind,
     To you and all mankind."

"To you, in David's town, this day
   Is born of David's line
The Savior who is Christ the Lord,
   And this shall be the sign,
     And this shall be the sign."

"The Heav'nly Babe you there shall find
   To human view displayed,
All meanly wrapped in swathing band
   And in a manger laid,
     And in a manger laid."

"Ail glory be to God on high,
   And to the earth be peace,
Good will henceforth from heav'n to men,
   Begin and never cease,
     Begin and never cease."

While Shepherds Watched Their Flocks

Nahum Tate   **Ravenscroft**

While shep-herds watched their flocks by night, All seat-ed on the ground, The an-gel of the Lord came down, And glo-ry shone a- round.

Through the year this day
of days
Brings to the heart again
An echo of the angel's song
Peace and good will to men